BUSINESS LAW

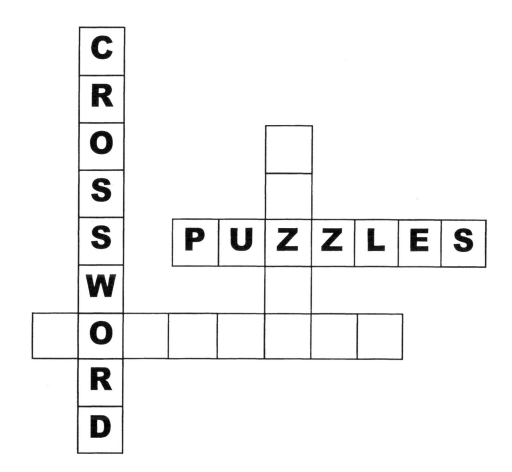

S. ANDREW OSTAPSKI

PRENTICE HALL
BUSINESS PUBLISHING

To my children, Victoria and Andrea, my wife, Maribel, and my parents, who taught me that learning works best when it is fun.

The Big Puzzle

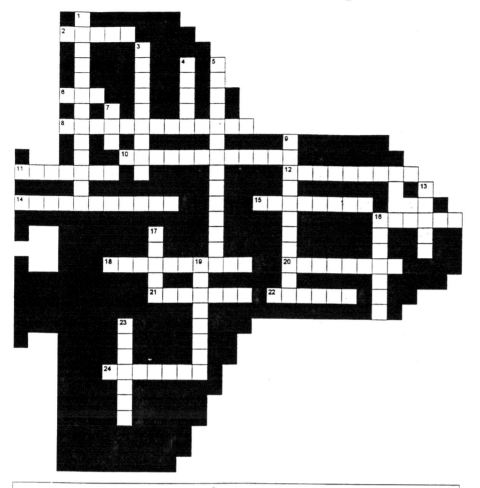

Across

2. UCC Article 2 applies to the sale of these things
6. Special-status transferee of a negotiable instrument (3 letters)
8. Level of evidence required for burden of proof in a civil case
10. Method principal later approves agent's unauthorized act
11. Requirement for a negotiable instrument
12. Are responsible for the corporation's overall policies
14. The LLC is treated like this entity for tax purposes
15. Parties must have this legal ability to form a contract
16. Known as the statutes of the corporation
18. When creditor has an enforceable security interest against debtor
20. Principle of appearance preventing principal from denying agency
21. Warranty arising from a sample as conforming to finished product
22. Principles that differentiate right from wrong
24. If the defendant fails to file an answer, this judgment may occur

Down

1. Something of legal value given in exchange for a promise
3. Body of law developed from judicial decisions (2 words)
4. Generally possesses the right to avoid liability under the contract
5. Bargain that is one sided, harsh and shocking to the conscience
7. Most states adopted this law on general partnerships (3 letters)
9. This contractor is not an employee but may be an agent
13. Rule 10(b)-5 prohibits this illegal activity
16. Laws regulate the sales of securities within a state (2 words)
17. Corporations are formed under the law of this political jurisdiction
19. Has special knowledge/skill of contract's practices or goods
23. In a limited partnership, this partner has unlimited liability

Basics of the Law

Down

1. body of law developed from judicial decisions (two words)
3. stare decisis
5. person filing the lawsuit
7. system that promotes social order and justice
9. this court may order specific performance

Across

2. legal reasoning that supports a court's decision
4. in a case at law, this remedy is awarded
6. establishes methods for enforcing rights (two words)
8. this court reviews the trial court's decision
10. principles that differentiate right from wrong

Ethics and Social Responsibility

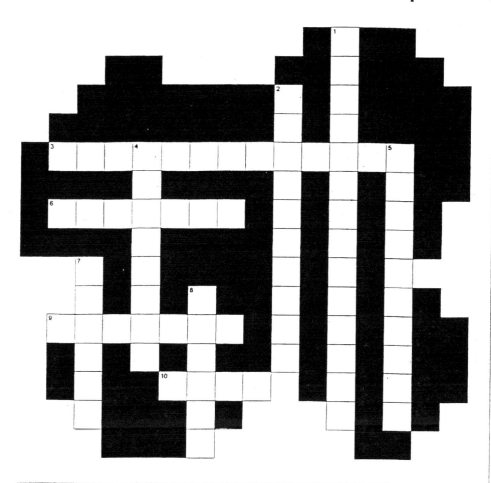

Down

1. Moral approach based on the consequences of an action
2. Philosophical system concerned with universal moral duties
4. A stakeholder that is affected by a business decision
5. Regulates business activity
7. Major motive for business activity
8. Sets a standard for determining right from wrong

Across

3. Employee's act of reporting illegal or immoral company activity
6. Interpersonal value that recognizes human dignity
9. Personal value which consists of candidness or openness
10. Believed decisions should be made based on their utility

Court System and Litigation

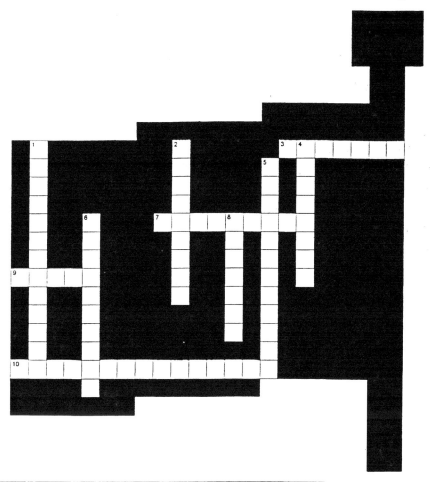

Down

1. level of evidence required for burden of proof in a civil case
2. process of obtaining information for a lawsuit
4. judges are selected either by merit or by this method
5. court has this power to decide a case
6. challenge & dismissal of juror without a stated reason
8. statute allows court to reach a defendant outside state (2 words)

Across

3. if the defendant fails to file an answer, this judgment may occur
7. this pleading sets out the reason for the lawsuit
9. particular geographic area where a lawsuit is brought
10. no minimum $ amount needed for such federal case (2 words)

Alternative Dispute Resolution

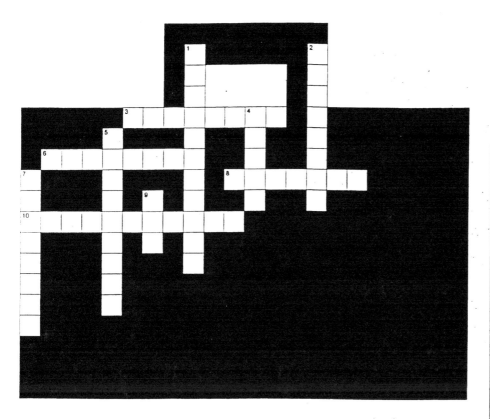

Down

1. Method for dispute resolution by an impartial third person
2. arbitration required by court
4. The arbitrator's decision
5. ADR method used in complex, commercial disputes
7. An arbitration clause may be found in this enforceable agreement
9. U.S. private, non-profit organization which administers arbitration

Across

3. UN agency that developed arbitration rules for international trade
6. Impartial third person who actively encourages parties to settle
8. Court documents are public but most ADR records are subject to
10. The most common form of informal ADR

The Constitution

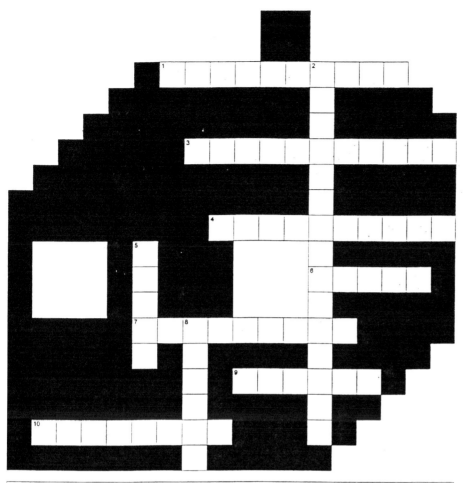

2. Requires gov. to treat similarly situated people similarly (2 words)
5. This amendment protects religion, speech, press & assembly
8. State possesses this power as part of its inherent sovereignty

Across

1. This amendment requires states to provide residents due process
3. Due process has two sides: procedural and this aspect
4. system of shared power between states and federal government
6. The federal government is divided into this number of branches
7. Clause prohibits state laws conflicting with exclusive federal law
9. Marbury v. Madison established this federal judicial power
10. This clause gives feds power over interstate movement of goods

Administrative Law

Down

1. Agency rules are available to the public through this source
2. Agency that regulates the broadcast media
3. Law setting procedures by which all federal agencies must act
6. One of the admin agency's prime responsibilities (2 words)
7. Congressional act which creates most administrative agencies
9. Case may be appealed to the judicial courts only after this occurs

Across

4. Programs that benefit the public at large (2 words)
5. The reduction of government regulation
8. Agency freestanding from the president and Congress
10. One goal of administrative law is this type of regulation

Criminal Law

Down

1. Delivery of accused to foreign place where crime occurred
2. Substantially likely that individual has committed a crime (2 words)
4. Crime punishable by confinement for up to a year
5. One of four categories of mens rea
6. Crime punishable by imprisonment for more than a year
9. Charge issued by a grand jury

Across

3. Pattern of racketeering activity (4 letters)
7. Process where illegal funds appear to be earned legally (2 words)
8. When a person agrees with one or more others to commit a crime
10. Amendment preserves right against self-incrimination

Torts

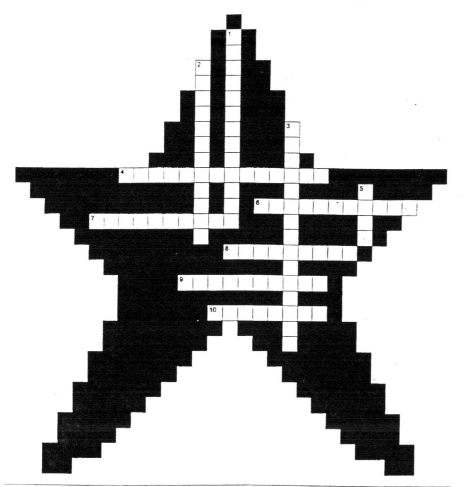

Down

1. Burden of proof in a tort case
2. Name of tort related to trademarks, patents and copyrights
3. Liability without fault (2 words)
5. Civil injury or wrong

Across

4. Test for proximate cause
6. Assault and/or battery is this type of tort
7. Type of tort that consists of harm caused by careless acts
8. Necessary element to establish negligence
9. Civil side of crimes related to stealing
10. Type of damages awarded in a tort case

Contract Formation

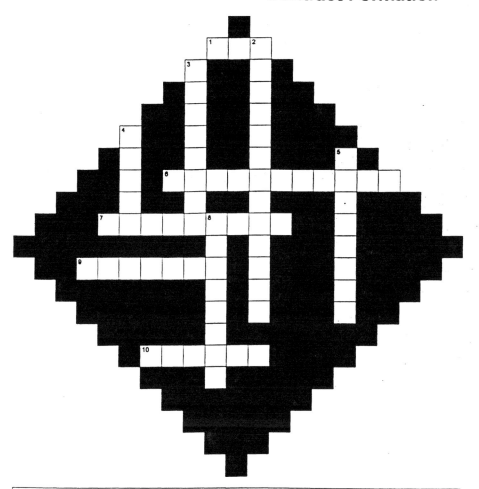

Down

2. Something of legal value given in exchange for a promise
3. Legally enforceable agreement
4. Contract by operation of law
5. Parties must have this legal ability to form a contract
8. A fully performed contract

Across

1. Codified statutes regulating commercial law in the U.S.
6. Source of commercial law (2 words)
7. Contract which is a "promise for a promise"
9. Party to whom offer is made
10. Forcing a party to enter an agreement by fear or threat

Contract Defenses and Remedies

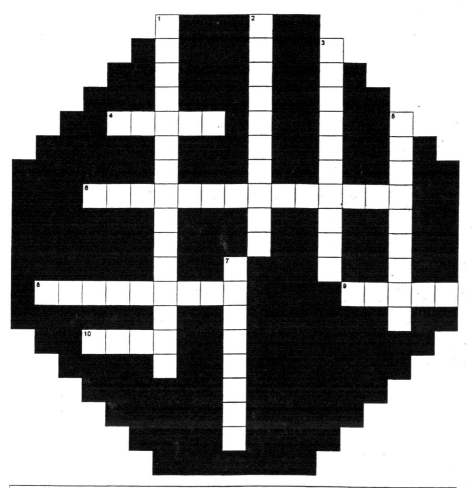

Down

1. Requires valid contract in writing for enforceability (3 words)
2. Transfer of duties to another person
3. Amount of damages agreed in contract in event of breach
5. One method by which a contract is discharged
7. A requirement for a valid contract

Across

4. Charging a higher interest on a loan than the law allows
6. Bargain that is one sided, harsh and shocking to the conscience
8. Remedies which are other than monetary damages
9. Generally possesses the right to avoid liability under the contract
10. Lack of regulatory license results in this type of business contract

Sales Law

Down

2. One of the most common documents of title (3 words)
3. UCC Article 2 applies to the sale of these things
5. Warranty arising from a sample as conforming to finished product
8. Buyer's remedy for breach of contract

Across

1. Commonly used shipping contract
4. Person with risk of loss can obtain this protection
6. Sale where purchaser may try goods for a reasonable time
7. Must pay shipping costs in point of shipment contract
9. A baker's dozen is an example of this UCC rule (3 words)
10. Has special knowledge /skill of contract 's practices or goods

Negotiable Instruments

Down

1. Two words normally associated with a qualified indorsement
4. An IOU is this type of instrument
5. One of three rules dealing with a basic theft by using a check
6. This draft is not payable on demand
9. Forgery is an example of this type of defense to avoid payment

Across

2. The effective period of months for a written stop payment order
3. Special-status transferee of a negotiable instrument (3 letters)
7. Person who has physical possession of the instrument
8. Example ot a two party instrument (2 words)
10. Requirement for negotiable instrument

Secured Transactions

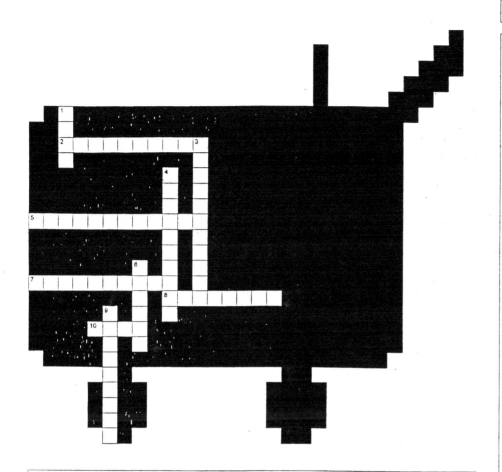

Down

1. Type of property excluded from UCC Article 9
3. Statement which shows that the debt has been paid
4. Judgment which creditor may obtain if loan balances are unpaid
6. One method of perfection
9. Statement that appears on a UCC-1 form

Across

2. When creditor has an enforceable security interest against debtor
5. Remedy available to secured party upon debtor's default
7. Procedures to protect creditor's rights over third parties' claims
8. Type of goods where perfection occurs automatically with PMSI
10. Common name for secured transaction

International Business

Down

1. Parent organization of International Court of Justice (2 words)
2. Organization oversees GATT & resolves trade disputes (3 letters)
4. Member of NAFTA (2 words)

Across

3. Method of financing international sale (3 words)
5. The political consolidation of European countries (2 words)
6. Shipment document that controls possession of goods (3 words)
7. Source of international law
8. Unfair import practice of selling below price
9. A general practice among nations which is accepted as int'l law
10. Tax placed on imported goods

Rights of Debtors and Creditors

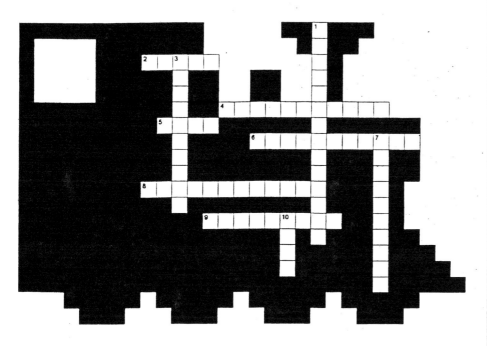

Down

1. Chapter 11 provides this relief for individual and business debtors
3. This Reporting Act regulates the credit reporting industry (2 words)
7. List of property that the debtor may keep from being liquidated
10. Requires disclosure of finance charge and APR (4 letters)

Across

2. Dollar limit of credit card holder's liability if card is lost or stolen
4. Process that takes place to assets in a Chapter 7 bankruptcy
5. Primary source of fed. law covering credit transactions (4 letters)
6. Procedure for seizure of debtor's bank account or wages
8. A debt that cannot be discharged in bankruptcy (2 words)
9. Writ allowing the seizure and sale of debtor's nonexempt property

Consumer Protection

Down

1. This regulation rule is a statement of law for general applicability
3. Exaggerated opinion expressed by the seller of the goods
4. Low price sales tactic designed to lure customers (3 words)
7. This advertising counters prior false advertising
9. What acts or practices are prohibited by the Wheeler-Lea Act

Across

2. State statutes that prohibit deceptive acts or practices (4 letters)
5. Federal agency concerned with consumer protection (3 letters)
6. An unsupported claim is an example of this kind of advertising
8. Magnuson-Moss establishes standards for this disclosure
10. The FTC can obtain an injunction from this U.S. body (2 words)

Property Law

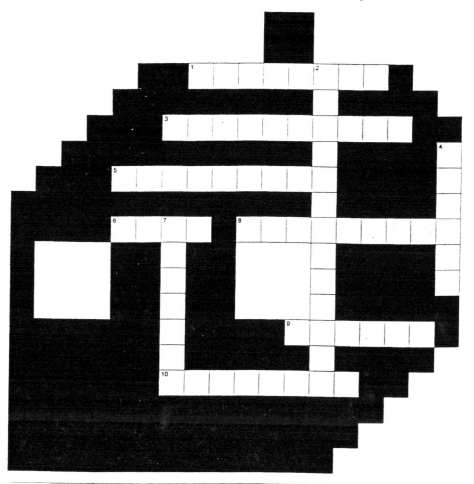

Down

2. Conversion of land to public use through police power (2 words)
4. Ownership passes to heirs, if interest is a tenancy in (1 word)
7. Possession that results in title to land without a deed

Across

1. One's delivery of personal prop. without transfer of title to another
3. Common stock or a check is an example of this type of property
5. Most complete form of ownership for title to land (2 words)
6. Property including land surface, below the surface, and airspace
8. Deed transfers whatever interest the grantor may have, if any
9. Exclusive right to an invention for seventeen years
10. Right to place electrical or telephone wires on another's property

Agency Law

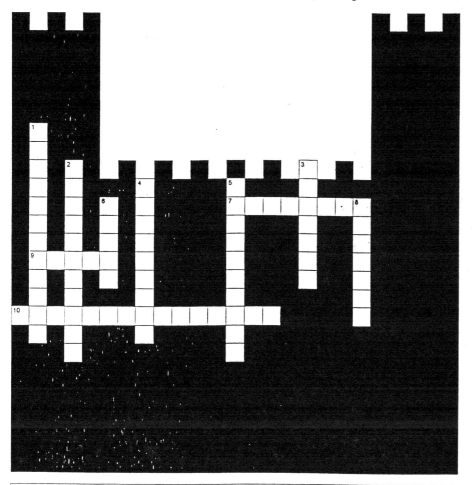

Down

1. Method principal later approves agent's unauthorized act
2. This contractor is not an employee but may be an agent
3. Actual authority can be either express or this type
4. Has the right to control the agent's conduct
5. The doctrine of respondeat superior is associated with this tort
6. Occurrence which immediately ends the ordinary agency
8. One of the agent's duties to the principal

Across

7. Principle of appearance preventing principal from denying agency
9. Agrees to represent or act on the behalf of another
10. Document grants authority to perform acts for another (3 words)

Noncorporate Business Entities

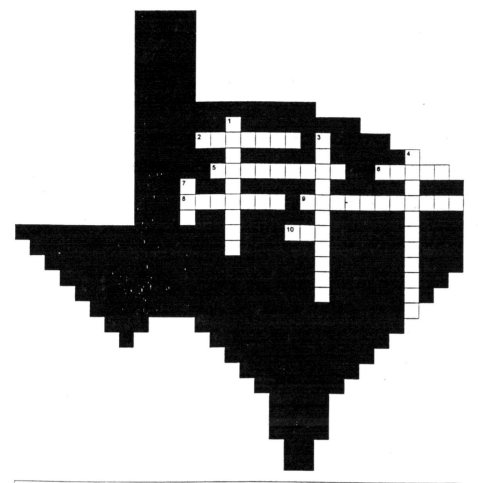

Down

1. A sole proprietor has this kind of liability
3. After partnership is wound up, process of assets distribution
4. The LLC is treated like this entity for tax purposes
7. Hybrid business form with limited liability & pass through (3 letters)

Across

2. In a limited partnership, this partner has unlimited liability
5. Each partner has this duty to act for the benefit of the partnership
6. Event that triggers partnership's dissolution
8. This partnership is authorized by statute
9. Partnership union is discontinued
10. Most states adopted this law on general partnerships (3 letters)

Corporate Law

Down

1. Court pierces this to take shareholders' personal assets (2 words)
2. Are responsible for the corporation's overall policies
4. A type of equity security (2 words)
5. Status allowing a corporation to be taxed as a partnership (1 letter)
10. Corporations are formed under the law of this political jurisdiction

Across

3. The people who start the corporation
6. Separate legal entity owned by shareholders
7. Makes contracts & takes initial steps to organize the corporation
8. Known as the statutes of the corporation
9. Conduct the corporation's day-to-day activities

Securities Law

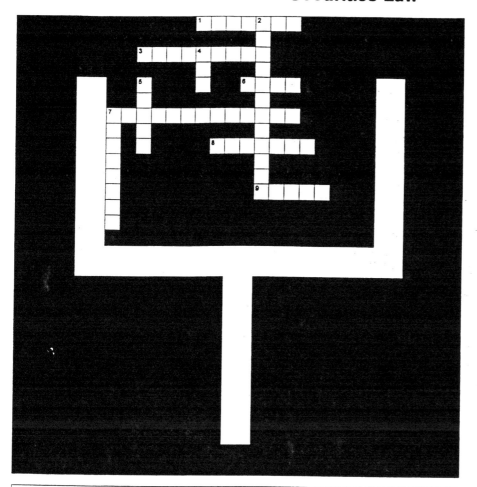

Down

2. Defense to liability for false statements under 1933 Act (2 words)
4. Federal body that regulates securities (3 letters)
5. Rule 10(b)-5 prohibits this illegal activity
7. Stocks and bonds are two common examples of this investment

Across

1. Section 16 of the 1934 act prohibits this type of trading
3. Written ad during 1933 Securities Act registration waiting period
6. Runs fund for harm caused when brokerage firms fail (4 letters)
7. One of three exempt transactions from registration (2 words)
8. Laws regulate the sales of securities within a state (2 words)
9. Name of SEC's electronic document filing system

Antitrust

Down

1. This price fixing is generally illegal per se
2. This rule determines if trade restraint is unreasonable (3 words)
6. First federal Act to promote competition within the U.S.
7. Robinson-Patman makes this discrimination illegal
8. Name of federal "trust busting" agency (3 letters)

Across

3. Business controls exclusively or near totally market share
4. Restraint of trade exists when this activity is substantially lessened
5. Professional sport exempt from the antitrust laws
9. Laws that regulate economic competition
10. Act which prohibits specific monopolistic practices

Labor Law

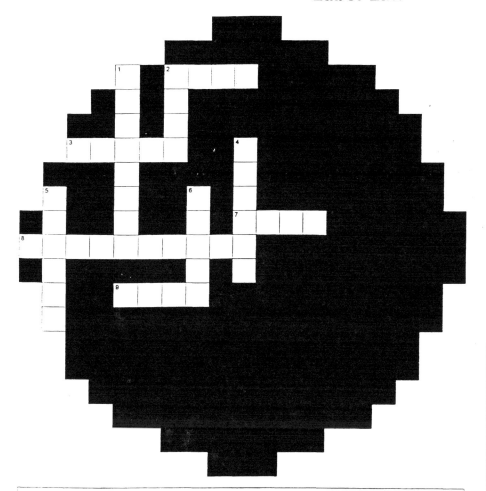

Down

1. One and one-half times the employee's regular wages
2. Established federal minimum wage requirements (4 letters)
4. Act that prohibits unfair labor practices by management
5. Taft-Hartley made these shops illegal
6. Legislation regulating retirement plans by employers (5 letters)

Across

2. Requires employees & employers to fund Social Security (4 letters)
3. Provisions constitute a "bill of rights" for union members (5 letters)
7. Federal agency involved with certification of unions (4 letters)
8. Bargaining that concerns terms & conditions of employment
9. Federal agency for workers' health & safety standards (4 letters)

Discrimination Law

Down

1. One of two kinds of sexual harassment (3 words)
2. Number of workers needed for Title VII to apply
3. One of two disparate theories to test if discrimination occurred
4. Act that protects persons with AIDS or cancer (3 letters)
7. Age at which person is protected by the ADEA
8. Environment in which sexual harassment exists

Across

5. Defense which allows discrimination (4 letters)
6. Action taken to remedy past discriminatory practices
9. Admin agency that enforces federal discrimination laws (4 letters)
10. The Civil Rights Act of 1964 prohibits discrimination on this ground

Environmental Law

Down

2. FEPCA controls the application of these products
4. NEPA requirement to assess impact of proposed action (3 letters)
5. Statute provides a tracking system for hazardous waste (4 letters)
9. The Endangered Species Act protects the species and this area

Across

1. Makes the rules for various federal environmental acts (3 letters)
3. Common law tort for unreasonable use of land adverse to other
6. The Solid Waste Disposal Act encourages this activity
7. Air standards adopted to protect the public health
8. Name of pollution effect that results in global warming
10. Requires cleanup of toxic hazardous sites

Course: _____
Term: _____

Instructor: _____
Name: _____

Business Law
The Puzzle Game
Performance Tally

Grader:										
Minutes:										
Points	Puzzle 1	Puzzle 2	Puzzle 3	Puzzle 4	Puzzle 5	Puzzle 6	Puzzle 7	Puzzle 8	Puzzle 9	Puzzle 10
10										
9										
8										
7										
6										
5										
4										
3										
2										
1										
0										

Scale:
0: Hopeless
1-2: Pitiful
3-4: Weak
5-6: Poor
7: Fair
8: Good
9: Excellent
10: Outstanding

Answers to Crossword Puzzles

The Big Puzzle

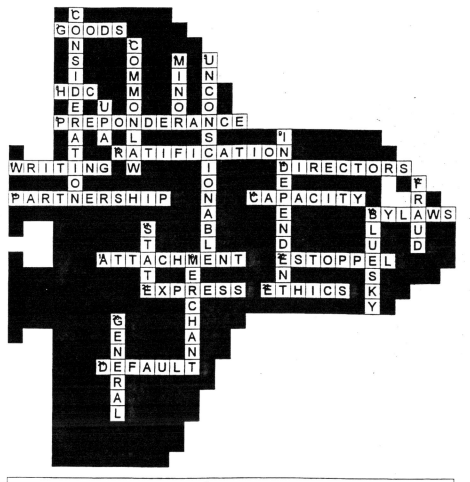

Across

2. UCC Article 2 applies to the sale of these things
6. Special-status transferee of a negotiable instrument (3 letters)
8. Level of evidence required for burden of proof in a civil case
10. Method principal later approves agent's unauthorized act
11. Requirement for a negotiable instrument
12. Are responsible for the corporation's overall policies
14. The LLC is treated like this entity for tax purposes
15. Parties must have this legal ability to form a contract
16. Known as the statutes of the corporation
18. When creditor has an enforceable security interest against debtor
20. Principle of appearance preventing principal from denying agency
21. Warranty arising from a sample as conforming to finished product
22. Principles that differentiate right from wrong
24. If the defendant fails to file an answer, this judgment may occur

Down

1. Something of legal value given in exchange for a promise
3. Body of law developed from judicial decisions (2 words)
4. Generally possesses the right to avoid liability under the contract
5. Bargain that is one sided, harsh and shocking to the conscience
7. Most states adopted this law on general partnerships (3 letters)
9. This contractor is not an employee but may be an agent
13. Rule 10(b)-5 prohibits this illegal activity
16. Laws regulate the sales of securities within a state (2 words)
17. Corporations are formed under the law of this political jurisdiction
19. Has special knowledge/skill of contract's practices or goods
23. In a limited partnership, this partner has unlimited liability

Basics of the Law

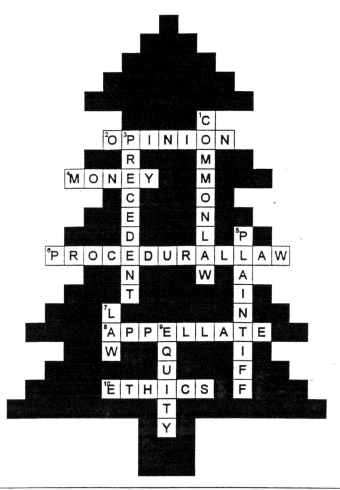

Crossword grid (tree-shaped):

- 2 Across: OPINION
- ¹C at top of COMMONLY column
- MONEY
- PROCEDURAL LAW
- APPELLATE
- ETHICS

Down words in grid: PRECEDENT, COMMONLY, PLAINTIFF, LAW, EQUITY

Down

1. body of law developed from judicial decisions (two words)
3. stare decisis
5. person filing the lawsuit
7. system that promotes social order and justice
9. this court may order specific performance

Across

2. legal reasoning that supports a court's decision
4. in a case at law, this remedy is awarded
6. establishes methods for enforcing rights (two words)
8. this court reviews the trial court's decision
10. principles that differentiate right from wrong

Ethics and Social Responsibility

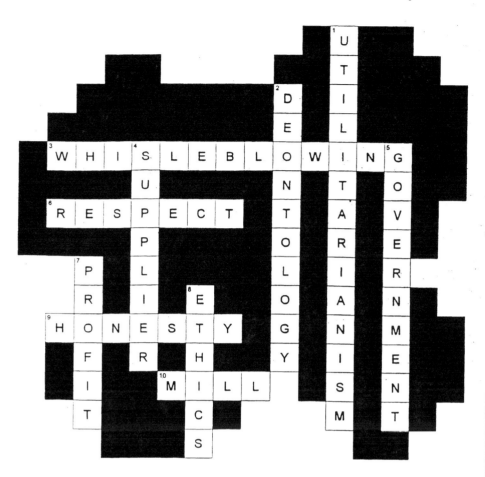

Down

1. Moral approach based on the consequences of an action
2. Philosophical system concerned with universal moral duties
4. A stakeholder that is affected by a business decision
5. Regulates business activity
7. Major motive for business activity
8. Sets a standard for determining right from wrong

Across

3. Employee's act of reporting illegal or immoral company activity
6. Interpersonal value that recognizes human dignity
9. Personal value which consists of candidness or openness
10. Believed decisions should be made based on their utility

Court System and Litigation

1 PREPONDERANCE
2 DISCOVERY
3 DEFAULT
4 ELECTION
5 JURISDICTION
6 PEREMPTORY
7 COMPLAINT
8 LONGARM
9 VENUE
10 FEDERALQUESTION

Across

3. if the defendant fails to file an answer, this judgment may occur
7. this pleading sets out the reason for the lawsuit
9. particular geographic area where a lawsuit is brought
10. no minimum $ amount needed for such federal case (2 words)

Down

1. level of evidence required for burden of proof in a civil case
2. process of obtaining information for a lawsuit
4. judges are selected either by merit or by this method
5. court has this power to decide a case
6. challenge & dismissal of juror without a stated reason
8. statute allows court to reach a defendant outside state (2 words)

Alternative Dispute Resolution

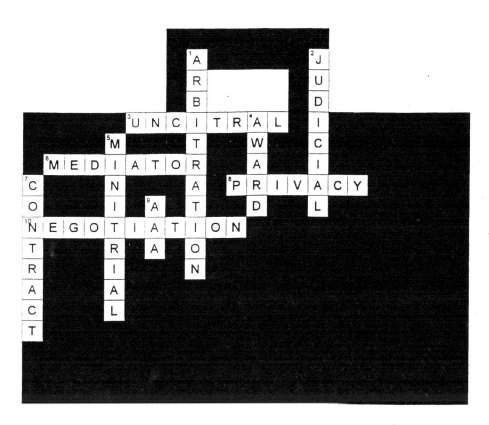

Down

1. Method for dispute resolution by an impartial third person
2. arbitration required by court
4. The arbitrator's decision
5. ADR method used in complex, commercial disputes
7. An arbitration clause may be found in this enforceable agreement
9. U.S. private, non-profit organization which administers arbitration

Across

3. UN agency that developed arbitration rules for international trade
6. Impartial third person who actively encourages parties to settle
8. Court documents are public but most ADR records are subject to
10. The most common form of informal ADR

The Constitution

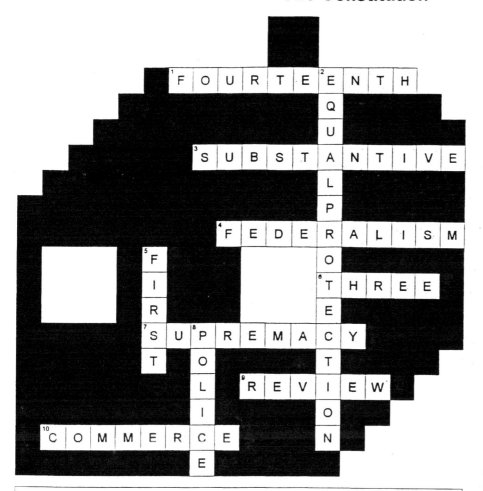

Down

2. Requires gov. to treat similarly situated people similarly (2 words)
5. This amendment protects religion, speech, press & assembly
8. State possesses this power as part of its inherent sovereignty

Across

1. This amendment requires states to provide residents due process
3. Due process has two sides: procedural and this aspect
4. system of shared power between states and federal government
6. The federal government is divided into this number of branches
7. Clause prohibits state laws conflicting with exclusive federal law
9. Marbury v. Madison established this federal judicial power
10. This clause gives feds power over interstate movement of goods

Administrative Law

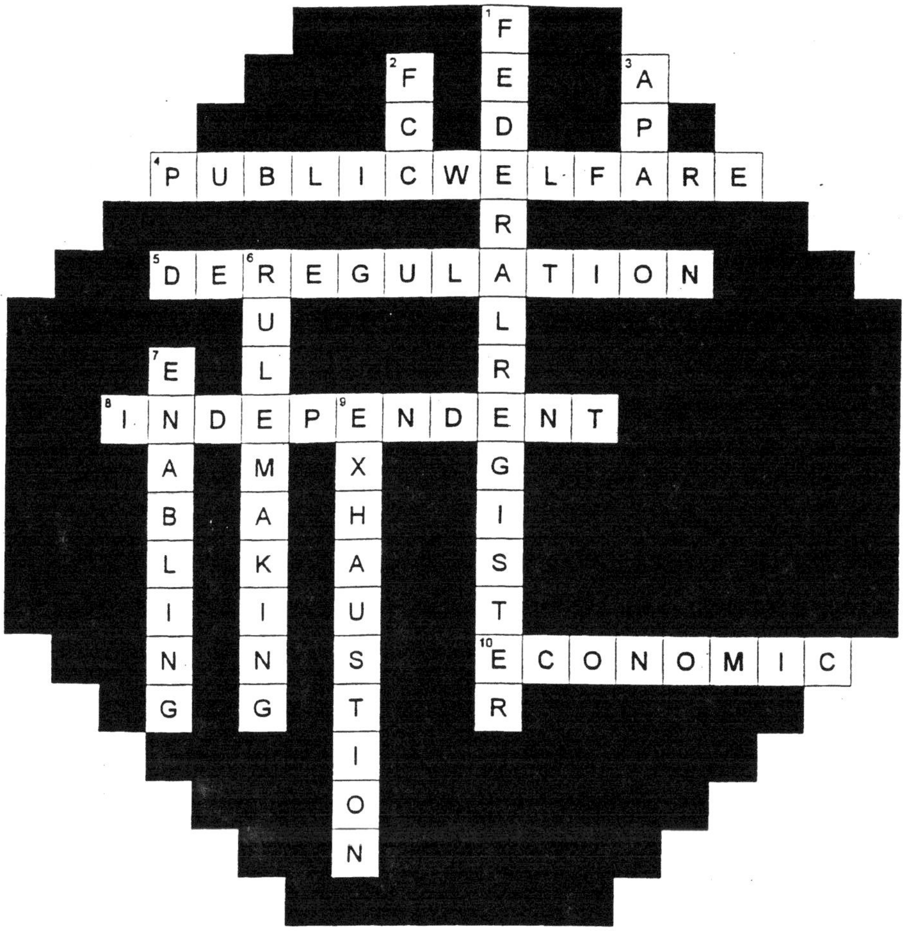

FEDERAL REGISTER
FCC
APA
PUBLIC WELFARE
DEREGULATION
RULEMAKING
ENABLING
INDEPENDENT
EXHAUSTION
ECONOMIC

Across

4. Programs that benefit the public at large (2 words)
5. The reduction of government regulation
8. Agency freestanding from the president and Congress
10. One goal of administrative law is this type of regulation

Down

1. Agency rules are available to the public through this source
2. Agency that regulates the broadcast media
3. Law setting procedures by which all federal agencies must act
6. One of the admin agency's prime responsibilities (2 words)
7. Congressional act which creates most administrative agencies
9. Case may be appealed to the judicial courts only after this occurs

Criminal Law

Down

1. Delivery of accused to foreign place where crime occurred
2. Substantially likely that individual has committed a crime (2 words)
4. Crime punishable by confinement for up to a year
5. One of four categories of mens rea
6. Crime punishable by imprisonment for more than a year
9. Charge issued by a grand jury

Across

3. Pattern of racketeering activity (4 letters)
7. Process where illegal funds appear to be earned legally (2 words)
8. When a person agrees with one or more others to commit a crime
10. Amendment preserves right against self-incrimination

Torts

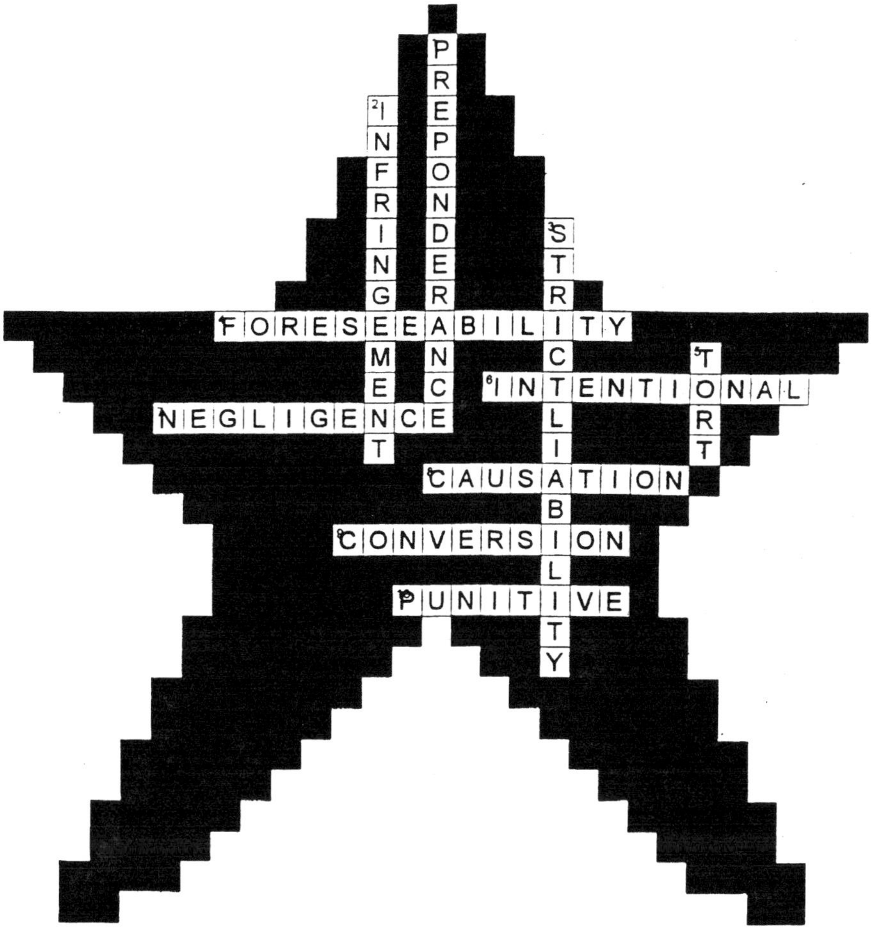

PREPONDERANCE
INFRINGEMENT
STRICTLIABILITY
FORESEEABILITY
TORT
INTENTIONAL
NEGLIGENCE
CAUSATION
CONVERSION
PUNITIVE

Across

4. Test for proximate cause
6. Assault and/or battery is this type of tort
7. Type of tort that consists of harm caused by careless acts
8. Necessary element to establish negligence
9. Civil side of crimes related to stealing
10. Type of damages awarded in a tort case

Down

1. Burden of proof in a tort case
2. Name of tort related to trademarks, patents and copyrights
3. Liability without fault (2 words)
5. Civil injury or wrong

Contract Formation

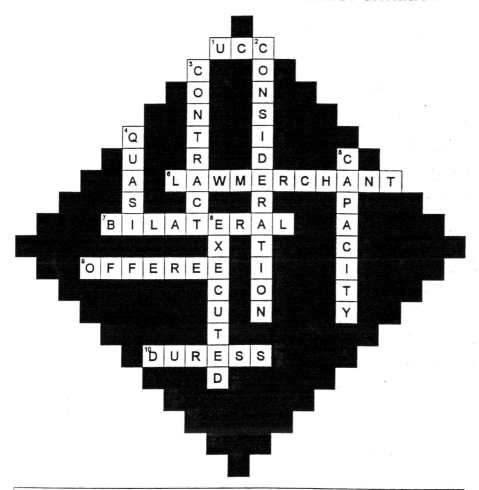

Down

2. Something of legal value given in exchange for a promise
3. Legally enforceable agreement
4. Contract by operation of law
5. Parties must have this legal ability to form a contract
8. A fully performed contract

Across

1. Codified statutes regulating commercial law in the U.S.
6. Source of commercial law (2 words)
7. Contract which is a "promise for a promise"
9. Party to whom offer is made
10. Forcing a party to enter an agreement by fear or threat

Contract Defenses and Remedies

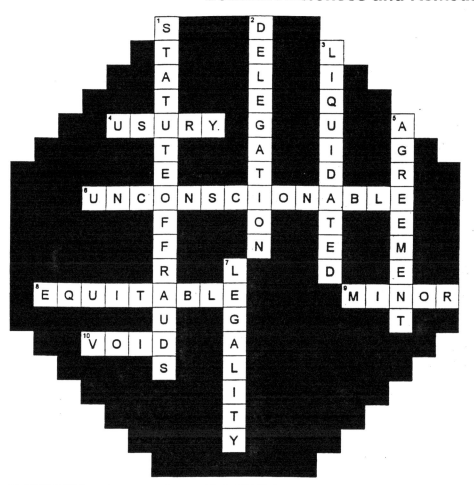

Down

1. Requires valid contract in writing for enforceability (3 words)
2. Transfer of duties to another person
3. Amount of damages agreed in contract in event of breach
5. One method by which a contract is discharged
7. A requirement for a valid contract

Across

4. Charging a higher interest on a loan than the law allows
6. Bargain that is one sided, harsh and shocking to the conscience
8. Remedies which are other than monetary damages
9. Generally possesses the right to avoid liability under the contract

10. Lack of regulatory license results in this type of business contract

Sales Law

The crossword grid contains the following answers:

Across:
1. FOB
4. INSURANCE
6. APPROVAL
7. BUYER
9. USAGE OF TRADE
10. MERCHANT

Down:
2. BILL OF LADING
3. GOODS
5. EXPRESS
8. COVER

Down

2. One of the most common documents of title (3 words)
3. UCC Article 2 applies to the sale of these things
5. Warranty arising from a sample as conforming to finished product
8. Buyer's remedy for breach of contract

Across

1. Commonly used shipping contract
4. Person with risk of loss can obtain this protection
6. Sale where purchaser may try goods for a reasonable time
7. Must pay shipping costs in point of shipment contract
9. A baker's dozen is an example of this UCC rule (3 words)
10. Has special knowledge /skill of contract 's practices or goods

Negotiable Instruments

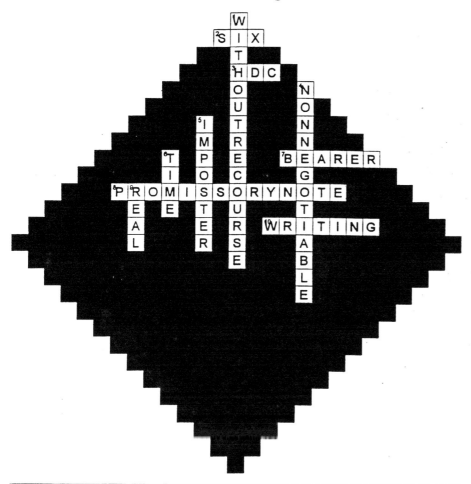

1. Two words normally associated with a qualified indorsement
4. An IOU is this type of instrument
5. One of three rules dealing with a basic theft by using a check
6. This draft is not payable on demand
9. Forgery is an example of this type of defense to avoid payment

Across

2. The effective period of months for a written stop payment order
3. Special-status transferee of a negotiable instrument (3 letters)
7. Person who has physical possession of the instrument
8. Example ot a two party instrument (2 words)
10. Requirement for negotiable instrument

Secured Transactions

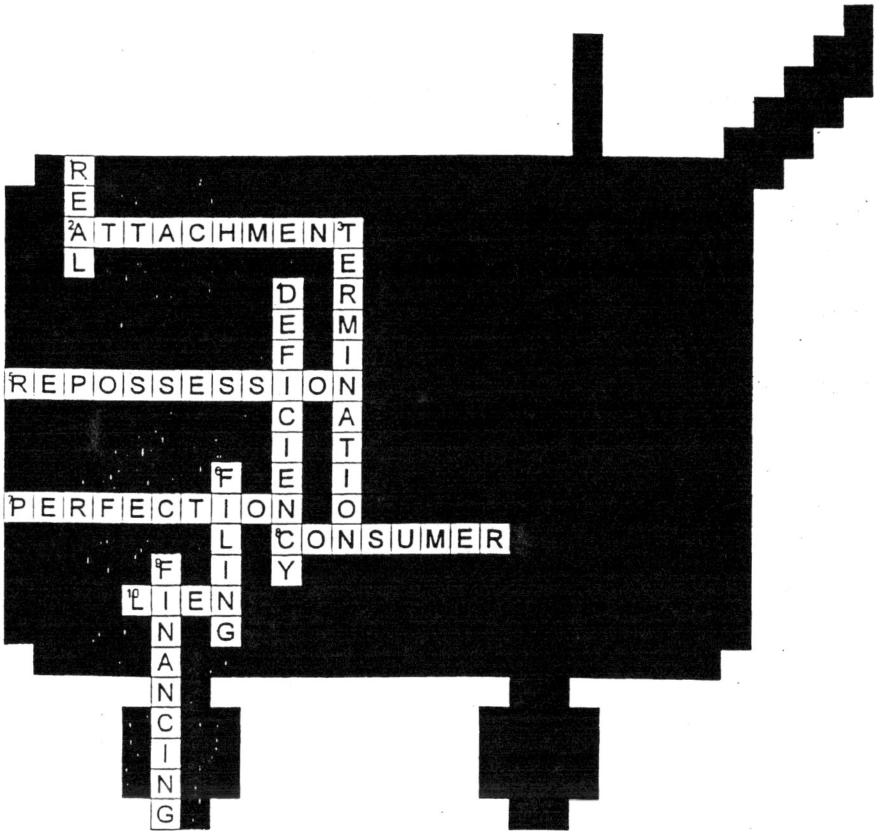

REAL
ATTACHMENT
TERMINATION
DEFICIENCY
REPOSSESSION
FILING
PERFECTION
CONSUMER
FINANCING
LIEN

Down

1. Type of property excluded from UCC Article 9
3. Statement which shows that the debt has been paid
4. Judgment which creditor may obtain if loan balances are unpaid
6. One method of perfection
9. Statement that appears on a UCC-1 form

Across

2. When creditor has an enforceable security interest against debtor
5. Remedy available to secured party upon debtor's default
7. Procedures to protect creditor's rights over third parties' claims
8. Type of goods where perfection occurs automatically with PMSI
10. Common name for secured transaction

International Business

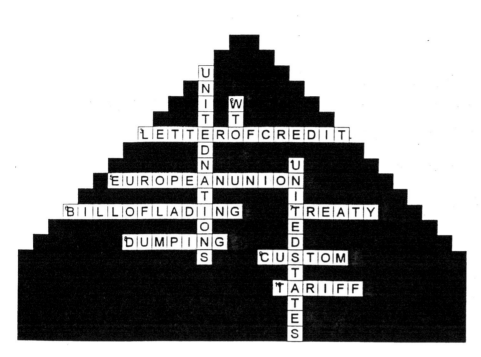

Down

1. Parent organization of International Court of Justice (2 words)
2. Organization oversees GATT & resolves trade disputes (3 letters)
4. Member of NAFTA (2 words)

Across

3. Method of financing international sale (3 words)
5. The political consolidation of European countries (2 words)
6. Shipment document that controls possession of goods (3 words)
7. Source of international law
8. Unfair import practice of selling below price
9. A general practice among nations which is accepted as int'l law
10. Tax placed on imported goods

Rights of Debtors and Creditors

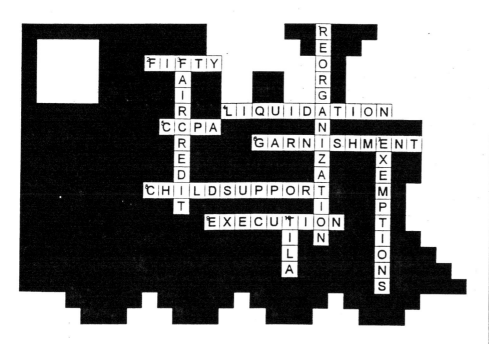

Down

1. Chapter 11 provides this relief for individual and business debtors
3. This Reporting Act regulates the credit reporting industry (2 words)
7. List of property that the debtor may keep from being liquidated
10. Requires disclosure of finance charge and APR (4 letters)

Across

2. Dollar limit of credit card holder's liability if card is lost or stolen
4. Process that takes place to assets in a Chapter 7 bankruptcy
5. Primary source of fed. law covering credit transactions (4 letters)
6. Procedure for seizure of debtor's bank account or wages
8. A debt that cannot be discharged in bankruptcy (2 words)
9. Writ allowing the seizure and sale of debtor's nonexempt property

Consumer Protection

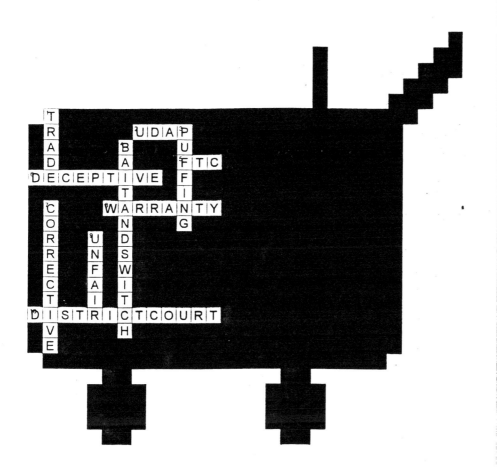

Crossword grid letters:
- T R A D (down, left)
- U D A P (across)
- D E C E P T I V E (across)
- B A T (down)
- P U F F I N G (down)
- F T C (across)
- C O R R E C T I V E (down)
- W A R R A N T Y (across)
- U N F A I (down)
- B A N D S W I T C H (down)
- D I S T R I C T C O U R T (across)

Down

1. This regulation rule is a statement of law for general applicability
3. Exaggerated opinion expressed by the seller of the goods
4. Low price sales tactic designed to lure customers (3 words)
7. This advertising counters prior false advertising
9. What acts or practices are prohibited by the Wheeler-Lea Act

Across

2. State statutes that prohibit deceptive acts or practices (4 letters)
5. Federal agency concerned with consumer protection (3 letters)
6. An unsupported claim is an example of this kind of advertising
8. Magnuson-Moss establishes standards for this disclosure
10. The FTC can obtain an injunction from this U.S. body (2 words)

Property Law

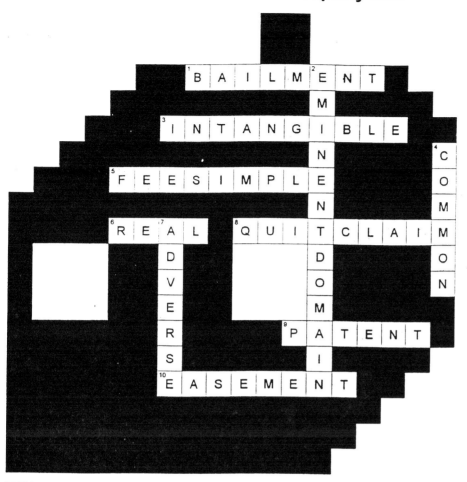

The crossword puzzle contains the following filled answers:

- BAILMENT
- INTANGIBLE
- FEE SIMPLE
- REAL
- QUITCLAIM
- PATENT
- EASEMENT

Down clue letters visible: EMINENT DOMAIN (crossing), CONDEMNATION, COMMON, ADVERSE

Down

2. Conversion of land to public use through police power (2 words)
4. Ownership passes to heirs, if interest is a tenancy in (1 word)
7. Possession that results in title to land without a deed

Across

1. One's delivery of personal prop. without transfer of title to another
3. Common stock or a check is an example of this type of property
5. Most complete form of ownership for title to land (2 words)
6. Property including land surface, below the surface, and airspace
8. Deed transfers whatever interest the grantor may have, if any
9. Exclusive right to an invention for seventeen years
10. Right to place electrical or telephone wires on another's property

Agency Law

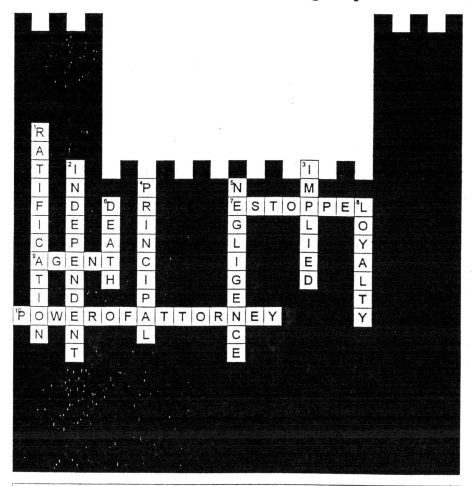

Down

1. Method principal later approves agent's unauthorized act
2. This contractor is not an employee but may be an agent
3. Actual authority can be either express or this type
4. Has the right to control the agent's conduct
5. The doctrine of respondeat superior is associated with this tort
6. Occurrence which immediately ends the ordinary agency
8. One of the agent's duties to the principal

Across

7. Principle of appearance preventing principal from denying agency
9. Agrees to represent or act on the behalf of another
10. Document grants authority to perform acts for another (3 words)

Noncorporate Business Entities

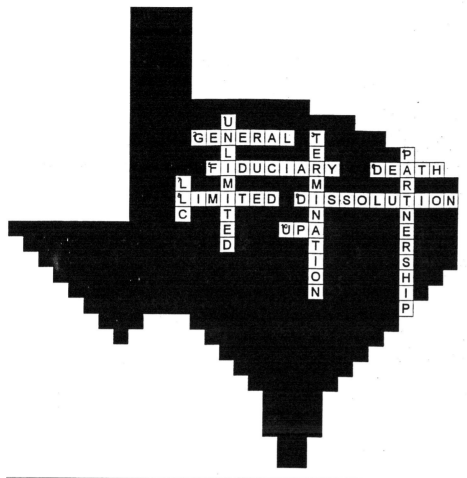

Down

1. A sole proprietor has this kind of liability
3. After partnership is wound up, process of assets distribution
4. The LLC is treated like this entity for tax purposes
7. Hybrid business form with limited liability & pass through (3 letters)

Across

2. In a limited partnership, this partner has unlimited liability
5. Each partner has this duty to act for the benefit of the partnership
6. Event that triggers partnership's dissolution
8. This partnership is authorized by statute
9. Partnership union is discontinued
10. Most states adopted this law on general partnerships (3 letters)

Corporate Law

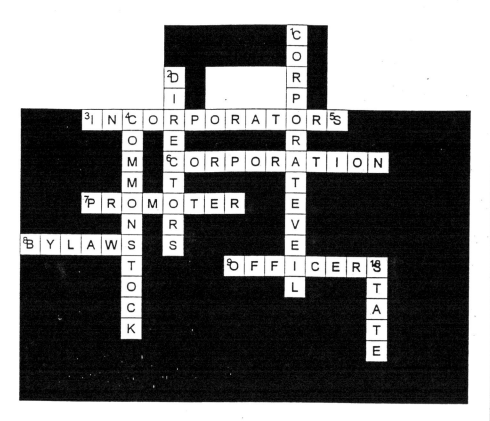

Down

1. Court pierces this to take shareholders' personal assets (2 words)
2. Are responsible for the corporation's overall policies
4. A type of equity security (2 words)
5. Status allowing a corporation to be taxed as a partnership (1 letter)
10. Corporations are formed under the law of this political jurisdiction

Across

3. The people who start the corporation
6. Separate legal entity owned by shareholders
7. Makes contracts & takes initial steps to organize the corporation
8. Known as the statutes of the corporation
9. Conduct the corporation's day-to-day activities

Securities Law

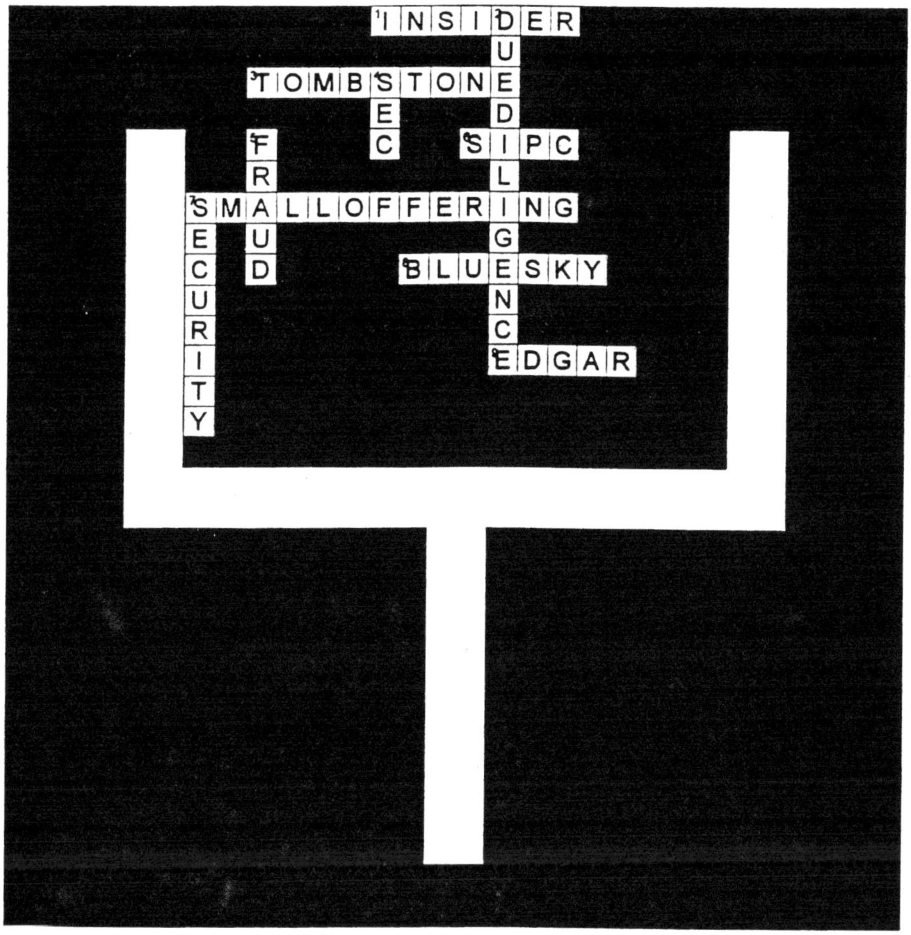

1 INSIDER
2 DUE DILIGENCE
3 TOMBSTONE
4 SEC
5 FRAUD
6 SIPC
7 SMALL OFFERING
7 SECURITY
8 BLUE SKY
9 EDGAR

Across

1. Section 16 of the 1934 act prohibits this type of trading
3. Written ad during 1933 Securities Act registration waiting period
6. Runs fund for harm caused when brokerage firms fail (4 letters)
7. One of three exempt transactions from registration (2 words)
8. Laws regulate the sales of securities within a state (2 words)
9. Name of SEC's electronic document filing system

Down

2. Defense to liability for false statements under 1933 Act (2 words)
4. Federal body that regulates securities (3 letters)
5. Rule 10(b)-5 prohibits this illegal activity
7. Stocks and bonds are two common examples of this investment

Antitrust

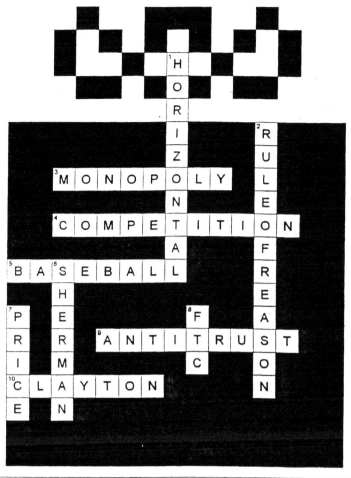

Down

1. This price fixing is generally illegal per se
2. This rule determines if trade restraint is unreasonable (3 words)
6. First federal Act to promote competition within the U.S.
7. Robinson-Patman makes this discrimination illegal
8. Name of federal "trust busting" agency (3 letters)

Across

3. Business controls exclusively or near totally market share
4. Restraint of trade exists when this activity is substantially lessened
5. Professional sport exempt from the antitrust laws
9. Laws that regulate economic competition
10. Act which prohibits specific monopolistic practices

Labor Law

Across

2. Requires employees & employers to fund Social Security (4 letters)
3. Provisions constitute a "bill of rights" for union members (5 letters)
7. Federal agency involved with certification of unions (4 letters)
8. Bargaining that concerns terms & conditions of employment
9. Federal agency for workers' health & safety standards (4 letters)

Discrimination Law

Down

1. One of two kinds of sexual harassment (3 words)
2. Number of workers needed for Title VII to apply
3. One of two disparate theories to test if discrimination occurred
4. Act that protects persons with AIDS or cancer (3 letters)
7. Age at which person is protected by the ADEA
8. Environment in which sexual harassment exists

Across

5. Defense which allows discrimination (4 letters)
6. Action taken to remedy past discriminatory practices
9. Admin agency that enforces federal discrimination laws (4 letters)
10. The Civil Rights Act of 1964 prohibits discrimination on this ground

Environmental Law

```
          ¹E  ²P  A
              E
      ³N  U  I  S  A  N  C  ⁴E
      ⁵R        T              I
  ⁶R  E  C  Y  C  L  I  N  G    S
      R        C
      A     ⁷P  R  I  M  A  R  Y
      A        D
⁸G  R  E  E  N  ⁹H  O  U  S  E
              A        ¹⁰S  U  P  E  R  F  U  N  D
              B
              I
              T
              A
              T
```

Down

2. FEPCA controls the application of these products

4. NEPA requirement to assess impact of proposed action (3 letters)

5. Statute provides a tracking system for hazardous waste (4 letters)

9. The Endangered Species Act protects the species and this area

Across

1. Makes the rules for various federal environmental acts (3 letters)

3. Common law tort for unreasonable use of land adverse to other

6. The Solid Waste Disposal Act encourages this activity

7. Air standards adopted to protect the public health

8. Name of pollution effect that results in global warming

10. Requires cleanup of toxic hazardous sites